THE TINY SHEEP

Illustrated by Bunshu Iguchi

What do you think? What will a man do who has one hundred sheep and one of them gets lost? He will leave the other ninety-nine grazing on the hillside and go to look for the lost sheep.

(Matthew 18:12)

Judson Press® Valley Forge

I am a tiny sheep.
I am the smallest one of a hundred sheep.
Everyone calls me "Teeny."
But I can run and jump faster than the others.

Our Shepherd is very kind. He watches us well.
Still, I must take care I am not left behind.
I am so small the Shepherd might not see me!

No, I should not be afraid.
Our Shepherd always cares about me.
I fell into the river last week.
Can you guess who saved me? The Shepherd!

Today we are going far away to a green hill.
We are all very happy. There is food ahead!

But the path is full of rocks. My feet hurt.
Blackie the crow comes to help me.
"Be brave, Teeny! Don't give up!" he says.
Blackie is my friend.

Here we are! My feet feel better now.
The green grass tastes good.
The flowers blow in the wind.
It feels nice here on top of the hill.

And now it is time to play!
I run and jump.
I smell the flowers and feel the wind.
Run, Teeny, run!
Have fun today!

Now I am all alone.
Even Blackie is gone.
The day is over.
Where am I?
Where is our Shepherd?

I am so tired! And I think I am lost.
Will the Shepherd notice?
I am so small. Will he miss me?

It is cold and dark.
I cannot walk anymore.
Will I *ever* see our Shepherd again?
What is that sound? Someone is coming!

It is our Shepherd! He is looking for me.
He did not forget me!
I was lost but now I am found.
He puts me on his shoulder. How sleepy I am....
I have never seen such a pretty moon....

"Tiny Teeny, tiny Teeny! Where have you been?
We missed you." Voices wake me up.
My friends welcome me back.

Now I am dreaming. In my dream
our Shepherd is with me.
And he will never leave me.

© 1985 Illustrations by Bunshu Iguchi
© 1985 Original story by Takeshi Sakuma
Originally Published in Japan by Shiko-Sha Co., Ltd.

© 1986 English text by Judson Press, Valley Forge, PA   19482-0851
Printed in Japan by the Toppan Printing Co./Osaka
ISBN 0-8170-1108-0

The name JUDSON PRESS is registered as a trademark in the U.S. Patent
Office.